ALL GROWN UP AND DRESSED IN WHITE

Memoirs By: Carrie G. (Ginny Girl) Kemp

ISBN: 1-4107-0922-1 (e-book)
ISBN: 1-4107-0923-X (Paperback)

Library of Congress Control Number: 2002096912

This book is printed on acid free paper.

Printed in the United States of America
Bloomington, IN

1stBooks – rev. 01/30/03

ACKNOWLEDGEMENTS

I am very grateful to many friends and family for the help that has been afforded to me while I have made the journey of writing these memoirs. However, there are also those who deserve special mention and therefore I offer thanks from my heart to my parents (deceased) first and foremost, to my siblings who provided some colorful parts of this story, and all the family and friends that have had to listen to my infamous phrase " I am going to write a book" for the past number of years, and wondered when I would produce. Most certainly, my husband and son who have spent many an hour watching me talk to the computer, to myself, and any other object that would listen when I felt the need to vent my frustrations.

Special acknowledgments go to Betty J. Patton,(my big sister) retired special education teacher, for assistance with editing the book. Cover design and creation – Anthony Quintanilla, Art Instructor, Holy Trinity High School, in Chicago, IL.

CONTENTS

INTRODUCTION

Having had the fancy to write a book or have my memoirs published about my desires and choices, which led me to a medical career, are the reasons for this exercise. It is hoped that the story will be interesting as well as informative and helpful to other minorities when making choices of a career just as I was able to do.

Hopefully as the story develops it can be ascertained the meager living my family experienced as I was growing up, and just how my parents sacrificed many things, many times for us children to have such good opportunities for education. One special incident or fact that comes to mind is the spending money I received every two weeks from home amounted to the grand total of $8.00 and was money momma received by laundering graduate nurses' uniforms, which she did for several of the graduates, who were on the nursing school faculty. Another interesting fact of interest is that I learned by chance somewhere along the way that Daddy's bi-weekly paycheck (take home pay) was equal to the amount I was making daily by the time I retired. Looking back at this fact, I realize how loving and giving my parents were. This paycheck of dad's took care of he and mother and 7 of us children. Mom and Dad were certainly the cream of the crop when I reflect on the amount of sacrifice and dedication that they possessed and practiced.

Mom and Dad were both natives of Alabama (they met in Indianapolis) and despite the many hardships encountered by them growing up, they always instilled only good thoughts in us and did not allow us to harbor bitter feelings regarding segregation and all the occurrences attached to the whole scenario. There are examples touched on in the book about how we encountered segregation on family trip to Alabama in 1949 to meet and visit the extended family, (what with no restrooms along the route to accommodate 'colored people' and how we made stops along the highway behind the billboards/bushes) and the time I drank 'white only' water while visiting my grandmother on another occasion makes for interesting reading. The most difficult situation for me to accept dealt with the treatment given the family when my maternal grandmother became ill and subsequently died. Because of the strength and quality of mom and dad's training I along with my siblings were able to overcome these situations as well as many others.

My support system other than my family for undertaking this project includes former patients, co-workers and friends. A more recent form of encouragement to proceed onward came from the delightful story by The Delaney Sisters with their book "Having Our Say", which was one of my retirement gifts from a co-worker. I also hope that some of the incidents experienced and related throughout the book are deemed as humorous as meant to be, since there is an effort made to pattern some of the writing after another favorite author of mine the late Erma Bombeck, and incidentally whose syndicated column several years ago was titled "Quit Dreaming of Authorship and Set Sail." This command was another incentive for me to get serious about writing my memoirs.

ADDENDUM TO THE INTRODUCTION

Since my original penning of the introduction there has been a very important and significant step taken in the lives of The Smith Siblings. This step being the development of 'THE ARCHIE AND BETTIE SMITH EDUCATION FUND, INC.' It has been a privilege thru the fund to give scholarship assistance to worthy students (academically eligible and financially in need) and desiring to attend a Catholic Junior High or Catholic High School. Besides giving their own personal donations to the fund, the family has been blessed with many friends who have helped sustain the fund.

The Smith Siblings express sincere thanks to anyone and everyone for their donations and continued support.

THIS BOOK IS THEREFORE DEDICATED TO BOTH

MOM AND DAD WITH LOTS OF LOVE ALWAYS.

PART I – GROWING UP

Carrie (Ginny Girl) Kemp

EARLY CHILDHOOD

I somehow can recall the location of my birthplace, but mostly from being informed by mom and dad. However, at the age of three and some change, moving day from that household is like an indelible mark in my memory bank. The house itself was the 'shotgun' version of a typical house/home for a family of our means. (The 'shotgun' home was one which when entered at the front door and you looked straight back, and whether or not you possessed good or mediocre eyesight, you could see all 4 rooms in the blink of an eye). Well, getting back to moving day, and there I was a 'busybody' 3 year old, who naturally was in the way and while the folks prepared items to be moved and gathered excess trash and other items doomed to be discarded rather than being moved on, (they were being

3

made ready for ye olde ragman to pick up as he traveled down the pathway right next to the back exit of the homestead. I almost became a statistic because I was too much underfoot and about to be run over by the ragman's wagon. This led to one of my more memorable spankings administered by mom and it was hardly forgotten. At this point I think poor mom would have severe charges of child abuse waged against her nowadays. Mom gave most of the spankings and dad gave out what I call generous doses of tongue lashings, which to me hurt just as bad if not worse. Don't get me wrong, dad did and could give out genuine punishment to the lower back side if he deemed it necessary. However, I think at this point there were no life long adverse reactions suffered by us children and truly thank my parents for the gifts given us as we grew up and thereby aiding us in becoming the productive persons we are and have been. Having survived this particular disciplinary action given by momma on moving day, the story continues and returns to the scene of the ragman and the other city workers responsible for helping keep the streets and the alleys of Indy in good clean shape. The ragman (an independent self-employed person) traveled about in an uncovered horse drawn wagon, the trash and garbage man were city employees and likewise had unique modes of transportation also horse drawn. The city wagons had large canvas type covers just like window shades used to cover the sides of the wagons whether the contents of the wagons were pure garbage with quite an odor, which could be strong since the garbage was collected sans plastic bags. The trash collection consisted of tin cans, newspapers, ashes (the residue from the coal burning furnaces) and the canvas like covers prevented these items from blowing in the wind and creating more trouble in trying to keep Indy clean.

Not long after the move a new baby arrived and the family now consisted of 4 girls and 1 boy. Our new house had all of 5 rooms, 2 bedrooms upstairs, and a living room, dining room (converted into a bedroom via a sleep sofa at night) a kitchen and bathroom (minus a bathtub) downstairs. There was also an unfinished basement. Our bath times were spent in the #10 tub in front of the potbelly stove, used for heating the house (before a fancy new coal burning furnace was installed in the basement as well as a bathtub being installed), but water was an expensive commodity and thus the #10 tub was the object of our affection on Saturday night, with heated water added at intervals for the next person's bath.

Mom and dad were both converts to Catholicism, so our education was in parochial schools. There was one parish for colored people, and that was located on the near east side of town, while the school was located on the west side. There was a Catholic Church and school in full view from our front porch, but the welcome mat especially for school was not rolled out to us until around 1949. This church and school ironically are now the location where the recipients of our scholarships and financial assistance are graduates. (My husband and I were married in the church.) Because of these above facts, we were bused to school in the very late '30's and early '40's. Now when I recall the distance of the church from our home it is real cause for amazement, since our family had increased by three children (2 more girls and a boy) while at this location, we managed or rather mom managed to have all of us up and ready for 6:00 A.M. Sunday mass without fail and this time table included travel time which enabled us to arrive no later than fifteen minutes prior to the start of mass. This sometimes even meant that the Smith Crew opened the church literally. Survival of this activity continued throughout the length of time our family resided at the current address. I think I was 6th or 7th grade before the parish church building next to our school on the west side was refurbished and remodeled and began having

Sunday masses on a regular basis and it became mandatory that all the school children attend 8:30 A.M. mass.

Some other memories, from the second home I resided in, are about the grocery shopping and the neighborhood itself. Grocery day was made very simple by the fact that we lived next door to the 'supermarket' and this building remains to be a food market some 60 years later. (It survived the wrecking ball, but our homestead did not) Shopping day was a truly family affair since $15.00 to $20.00 dollars spent required 4 or 5 of us to carry the groceries home next door. I also remember that we (the children) went to the rear door of the market and were treated to the throw away items mostly parts of the chicken deemed not for sale, and these parts were the liver and gizzards and the necks and backs. Little did we know what expensive eating we were able to partake of in the good ole days. Just think about it, chicken liver is now considered a delicacy costing almost as much as the whole chicken. Our eating was of course plain and simple, a lot of boiled food and then stretching the meal out with the ever- filling staple of rice, beans and the likes. ("We were poor,") but didn't know it, therefore very happy.

Many other things are recalled about our days of living in this particular house, things like the shady trees lining each side of the street, which seemed to aid in keeping us cool in the hottest of summer, and also gave an overall serenity to the neighborhood. There's a story which gives the details all about our short period of pet ownership – we children had a dog for 6-10 weeks when the puppy was apparently poisoned and died. There is the time my deceased brother and I were playing in our pre-school days and he befriended a stray cat. Well, my playmate became quite ill (not sure of cause) soon after his contact with the cat, and I imagine this probably figured in my discomfort with the feline family as well as other incidents, which created my fear of cats. It was common knowledge that my maternal grandmother did not care for cats herself. We did give the pet ownership one more shot but this dear dog was struck by a car, and died a few days later on my brother's birthday. He was devastated and the unanimous decision was made for no more pets. My earlier comments about the shady trees keeping it cool, brings to mind the ever so faithful icebox and the manner our food was kept refrigerated. The icebox provided us an additional chore, that of keeping the drip pan emptied, and keeping track of how much ice was left over and how much was to be purchased on the iceman's (a neighbor) next delivery day. The ice was sold in 25lb increments and there was a special card with different weight amounts printed out, and you simply placed the card in your window as to how much was needed. Our family had developed friendship with many other families living close by, as well as those living in the next block. One of the couples was our godparents, and in fact our godfather lived many years longer, he died at the age of 103 years old in the 1990's.

Other happenings of interest while living here were a visit from my paternal grandmother and a half sister from Alabama. Grandma was a 'little but mighty' individual and because of my age during this time details of the visit are very sparse in the memory bank, but I do recall what a treat it was to have company come visit with us. Mother's youngest brother and a cousin lived with us for a short period when both men ventured north to seek work and soon were drafted into WWII. My uncle lived with us when he was discharged, and because their discharges were at different times, the cousin found other living quarters close by and soon married and started his own family. A surprising revelation occurred recently, when my oldest sister received a letter from a probable cousin who traced her via the computer. Well because family is important we are in touch with more of our extended family. That cousin turned out to be a daughter of the cousin who lived with us when he first moved to Indianapolis.

It soon became time for a move since the family now numbered nine. The new house was a two-story house with four bedrooms, and a large yard for our playing activities. Moving day arrived and was carried out during the day while most of us were in school, and I am sure the plan called for this to avoid moving day interference from yours truly now all of 8 years old. The school bus driver was even in on the conspiracy and he knew to let us off the bus at the new address. Once the Oohs and Aahs were expressed and our excitement began to settle down, the question of who was going with daddy to close out the empty house and who stayed to help mother get things more in order for some facsimile of comfortable living. (I did get to go with daddy, and it created a great deal excitement just to see the old homestead empty of furniture). Helping dad turn off the utilities and being sure the windows and doors were locked securely made me feel like such a big helper.

There is some uncertainty in my memory when this move took place, but it was in the fall of 1942 or early spring 1943. At any rate, the wheels began turning to point me in the direction of being " All Grown Up and Dressed In White". The complete family consisted of another boy born in late summer 1943 and another girl born in 1951. They will be introduced down the road in this story.

THE FIRST JOB

The bright yellow school bus wound its way homeward on the usual route one particular slightly overcast day in April, but for two passengers it did not seem to move quite fast enough.

I was almost nine years old and my brother was 71/2 years old. We were to start our 'new jobs', which would have a significant impact on my career choice. Our new jobs were that of the papergirl and paperboy in the immediate neighborhood and one of the local hospitals, also in the neighborhood. The hospital was daddy's place of employment for the past 17 years and the next 24 years. He worked a total of 41 years and about eight months at the hospital. He during that time did help several members of our family and of course all of us children except the youngest work in some capacity during our growing up years at the hospital. Incidentally the baby girl was a teen volunteer. So in reality all of us had exposure to working and earning our spending money very early in our lives.

Me, myself and I being all of 4 feet 6-7 inches tall and at times being overshadowed by the red wagon full of evening papers, especially on the days of excessive advertisements was an unusual sight from the beginning. This union or combination lasted several years, which in reality terminated in August of 1952 just prior to my entering nursing school. Those nine years will always live in my mind.

The price of the daily paper was 4 cents per copy at the onset and   cost all of 5 cents when I retired my selling rights to the two younger girls to pursue my career in nursing.

Number eight sibling was soon due, and was born the summer of 1943. The oldest daughter now 13 years old was a big helper to mother when the baby arrived. She also embarked on her first job for pay (of course this being before enactment of child labor laws) at the hospital where I had the evening paper route and dad's place of employment in one of his many jobs, for instance he was a porter, general houseman, and during this time was the 'second string' chauffeur for the nuns along with other duties which included keeping the soda pop machines stocked, assisting the patients to their assigned area (room or ward assignments) following their admission procedures. Watching dad do his duties, sometimes caused both my brother and myself to be a little late sometimes. The family home was about 2 blocks from the hospital if the short cuts were not used. This in it self helped tremendously in respect to the need for transportation of the paper carriers, and now both of the two older girls were working in the hospital. Mom was free of being a part time chauffeur, which I doubt she would have ever become, because she refused to learn to drive for many reasons unlike all six of her daughters who were each one ready to learn to drive and did so by the age of 16. Mom confessed in later years, she felt responsible for an accident her brother had while driving daddy's car. Therefore, no driving lessons or driving for her. My two older sisters like daddy performed several jobs during their employment days at the hospital and to mention a few they were food servers, dishwashers, elevator operators, central supply aides and surgical aides. Of course relief paper carriers when needed.

The paper routes flourished both in the hospital sales, and the number of neighborhood customers. The excitement of selling the EXTRAS (papers used to cover stories about unusual happenings) was long remembered. Such events that I readily recall were the death of President Franklin D. Roosevelt, Truman's victory over Dewey in 1945 and 1948 respectively, and of course pre-television days, special sporting events especially those like the 500 Mile Race Day results and other activities surrounding the celebration.

The first job really was a real catalyst for me and helped me in making a decision in regards to what I would I wanted to be when I grew up. There were several afternoons I would or could be found located near the side entrance of the hospital counting my papers and engaging in conversation with nurses who had come to know me and also were regular customers. One particular day happened to be graduation day for the nurses. The ceremony was held in the hospital chapel, and the graduates in their crisp white uniforms (having spent three years in the stripped smocks and white pinafores) were a sight to behold. This was especially so for one little papergirl with eyes as big as saucers. In addition to the crisp uniform they had beautiful ribbons of blue and gold (the graduation colors flowing from the left side of the uniform with the school pin prominently displayed for all to see and to know that they had accomplished the goal of being a graduate nurse.

Many a 4th grader doesn't think in terms of his/her career choice, but believe me I did, and I announced my intentions to my parents that day after witnessing the graduation day excitement and activities. I plainly stated, "When I grow up, I want to be like those pretty ladies in white, thus the title of this book. A rather ironic incident occurred many years later when I was taking care of a prominent Black Attorney, who passed on my shift. It was revealed in an article written in the newspaper depicting his rise through the ranks in attaining his goal of being a lawyer. He also was nine years old and a 4th grader when he made his choice of a career, which turned into a very positive situation both for him, his family and his future. It was just about then, (which in reality is over 20 years ago) that the antennae in me began to make an ascent in the direction of writing a book. There was more fuel for the fire in me to write about my choices when not too long ago I learned of another person's choice being made at the age of nine and this individual is none other than the most successful and winning coach of Grambling University Mr. Eddie Robinson.

Well with my decision made and ready to take on the nursing profession, I felt the natural thing about nursing was helping people, and many an afternoon found the aspiring nurse being a people helper and getting into trouble by 'helping' and not 'selling' to the patients and of course raising the ire of a few other patients (who pre-television) depended on the evening paper being sold/delivered on time. So I found ways to keep most everyone happy by learning to deliver and sale the papers before I began being an official people helper by running errands or just visiting with them and doing other things permitted by someone of my size and capabilities.

SOME OF LIFE'S ADVENTURES

My brother and I took part in several contests for the paper carriers, and with our efforts our daily sales increased as well as the number of home delivery customers. We were rewarded as winners in one contest a trip to Cincinnati, Ohio to spend the day at Coney Island Amusement Park. I faintly remember how upset one of the chaperones was on the day of the trip,(which was on a Sunday thus no paper routes to be delivered). Well his being upset involved the fact 'Colored People' were not allowed to go to Coney Island Park and they were (that was my brother and I) were 'subjected' to attending a baseball game at Crosley Field. Well that made us like a character from the movie titled "Song of The South", more specific like Brer' Rabbit when he begged not to be thrown into the briar patch, knowing all along that action suited him just fine. It was just fine for us, because of our being a baseball oriented family and it did not hurt our feelings one bit. To coin a phrase, the score was 1 to 0 in our favor. The trip was enjoyed by one and all, and no one suffered from the change of destination for the 'Colored People' on the bus.

A few words about our baseball orientation can be recalled with a great deal of fondness. A special affordable treat for the family was an evening of baseball at the minor league home field –Victory Field. The ball field served as the home field of The Indianapolis Indians and the Indianapolis Clowns (The Negro League) to play occasional games. Beginning around 1948 our vacation was attendance (once or twice during the summer) at a major league game either in Cincinnati, Ohio or Chicago, Illinois mainly to see Jackie Robinson play when the Brooklyn Dodgers were playing either The Cubs or The Reds. Naturally, the trip was on a Sunday, because as mentioned earlier, no papers had to be delivered on Sundays. Our Sunday morning began around 2:00 A.M. so that we would arrive in the big city in time enough to 'find' the Catholic Church for mass, vintage 6:00 A.M. During this time in church history the mass was already in Latin (prior to Vatican II), but we managed to find a German, Polish, or Italian speaking parish church each time. Our obligation was made regardless. Then it was back to the car for an egg sandwich, which mom and dad had so lovingly prepared around 1:00 A.M. before we were awakened. The sandwich was eaten ala natural (oh what would not have been given for the sight of the Golden Arches or real modern day convenience of a microwave oven). The next task was that of finding our way to the ballpark, which always presented a small problem, since we did not attend the same church on each trip. Once this was accomplished we stayed close to the car until time for the park to open. The wait to enter the ballpark usually was 2-3 hours. Mass, breakfast and a pit stop (to accommodate 10 people) consumed about 2 hours and the remaining hour was spent praying for a rain free day. Out of all the many trips we made, I can recall only having our outing cut short by rain on one occasion. One might ask just why do I remember such an incident? Well, from that trip on and any others we took dad never worried about me getting lost from the family ever again. I became separated during the exodus one Sunday on a rainy day, and I having remembered where the car was parked, naturally headed straight for the car and had a bit of a wait for the rest of the family to arrive only without dear daddy. He was still searching for me. Once the family was happily reunited, the long drive home began with what I called dad's genuine tongue lashing. When I say dad did not worry about me from then on, I am serious and quite often in my adult days, he would expect me to have directions in the memory bank or at least be aware of the location of certain places and times.

As mentioned in the introduction, mom and dad were both natives of Alabama, and were very careful and protective of us children. With their actions of love and support we were able to avoid harboring any bitterness or unkind feelings associated with segregation such as the Coney Island Bus Trip for the paper carriers. As I look back now most of the incidents passed by without any visible scars, but they certainly represent a 'gone, but not forgotten' attitude. I certainly consider mom and dad as doing a wonderful job as the nine of us grew up. We were given a small preview of life in the south when the family took an unprecedented auto trip to Alabama. Before telling about the family trip, mention must be made of my first adventure to the southland by train with my own money. Travel by train was certainly the elite way to go in the 40's and the hustle and bustle at Union Station surrounding 'The South Wind' (name of the train we rode to Alabama) was very exciting. Around 1944 the family became a proud possessor of a telephone. Yes here we were phone owners, and even had only a two-party line. The party line indicated that each time the phone rang it was not always for your family to answer, but there were codes (1 long ring or 2 short rings) that determined each family's phone call. Well at the very grown up age of 10years, I decided to look up the phone number for the train station and inquire about the cost of a round trip ticket for a 10 year old from Indianapolis, IN to Decatur, AL. Upon being informed of the cost for the ticket (which was$9.00 and some cents), I immediately began saving for my ticket, in hopes of making the trip with momma, who made an annual trip to visit her mother (sans children). My grandmother for whom I was named made it that much more special for me to be able to make the trip. One day when I heard my parents talking over the plans to buy momma's ticket, I sprang the question on them about my chances of making the trip this year. Of course they both agreed that it would be too expensive. With that reply, I presented them with my 'mustard jar' bank with the needed monies for my ticket. This was "an offer they couldn't refuse". One slight problem arose from their decision for me to go on the trip, and of course that dealt with the paper route being taken care of during my absence. It was not long before matters were ironed out and the duties were to be shared with the other siblings and of course dear daddy. As best recalled, the trip covered the better part of a week.

This was one week that my poor grandmother wished had never occurred I am sure. You see, I became a modern day Jane Pittman, unintentionally of course. At this particular time in the midst of World War II it had become customary seeing signs in stores which limited the amount of certain items one could purchase and also whether or not

'Ration Stamps' were required as part of the purchase price. Well, while shopping on Bank Street with my dear grandmother, I became thirsty and spotted the water fountain. There was a sign above the water fountain (partially covered) which to my wandering eyes clearly stated ONLY, which I just knew referred to the number of packages of the cashew peanuts that could be purchased. However, it was discovered after I drank the water, the sign stated 'FOR WHITE ONLY'. My literally and figuratively frightened grandmother immediately paid for her purchases (never did find out if she was finished shopping) and grabbed me under the arm and I don't think my feet touched the ground for the two and one half block distance back to her home. Of course I received another one of those tongue lashings (those punishments I had grown to dislike). This was the only sour note during my 'mustard jar' bank trip to visit my grandmother. The good home cooking was exceptional and I really had royal treatment especially since

Carrie (Ginny Girl) Kemp

I was her namesake, and the fact that I saved up money to pay for my trip. A family reunion in 1997 found us housed in a hotel that practically stands on the hallowed grounds of where I stayed with my grandmother on that infamous trip in 1944. The hotel naturally is very close to the building, which housed the general store with 'THE WHITE ONLY ' water fountain. This and other revelations really made that family reunion special to me.

May 1949 was the year for the family trip to visit the grandmothers (both of them widowed) and to meet other relatives. The opportunity for the trip was to take place over a five-day weekend recess. During this time Ascension Thursday was not only a holyday of obligation, but a free day from school also, and special permission was given to us to be absent from school on the following day (Friday) and the long weekend was still extended to include Monday, May 30th (Memorial Day) already a free day. Well we set out bright and early Thursday following attendance at 6:00 A.M. mass for the holyday. Our travels were in a 1948 4-door Dodge Sedan to accommodate the family of ten. The children ranged in age from 19years old down to 4 years old and we did fit. Although the trip was a lengthy one, the seating arrangements were as follows; Dad, the oldest girl(who was now married and expecting her first child in the fall) and my bigger brother(not older than me just bigger and had longer legs) in the front seat. Dad was the only driver, since a pregnant woman driving was mostly unheard of, and my brother not old enough. Mom and the other six of us children filled out the back seat along with two small side seats created for the two younger boys ages seven and four years old and the life-saving portable potty chair for the younger ones unaccustomed to road side stops (behind billboard signs and in the bushes) these stops were necessary because of segregation policies for restrooms along the way. Restaurant policies also made eating stops more or less a roadside picnic. Mom and dad to the rescue once again, by making sandwiches with some of us helping and some of us being too helpful (yours truly was a big helper by this time). We also had to be innovative in preparing liquid refreshments, because gasoline stops were just for that – gas and nothing else. I am certain you can read between these lines. (We could not purchase cold drinks or other snacks if available at the gasoline stations). The trip took between 10-12 hours, what with speed limits, two-lane highways and of course automobile horsepower. Maternal grandmother's home was the 1st stop, we slept on chairs, couches, floor pallets, and mom and dad were in the extra bedroom. One can only imagine what a shock for my grandmother to wake up the next morning with ten visitors in her generally quiet and subdued home watching and waiting for breakfast. Grandma fixed a very delicious meal and much to our wonderment, she prepared the whole breakfast on and in her wood burning stove. The city where we spent the first night was pretty much like home and after breakfast there were a lot of grandma's friends coming by to see all eight of her grandchildren here to visit. We soon embarked upon the next leg of the trip and we headed further south. After another 150-175 miles we prepared to meet a lot more relatives and also see our paternal grandmother. One can just about imagine the number of relatives, when consideration that dad was the youngest of nine children and mom was one of three children.

The Good Lord smiled on us with good weather, and the family picnic planned out in the country for Saturday along with an old fashion baseball game (there goes another reference to our being well indoctrinated with baseball). Besides watching the ballplayers, yours truly was being a typical teenager busy looking over all the young boys. Well the discouraging fact to be revealed was that all the interesting and nice looking young boys were, you guessed it cousins. As adults there have been times for reminiscing and laughter, especially when attending family reunions. The fun and activity of Saturday afternoon was briefly interrupted when the two youngest brothers disappeared. They were found unharmed wandering in the nearby woods, having lost directions. There was a large snake spotted in the woods not too far from them, but no one was injured. Although not much was detailed about our Friday night, we did begin meeting many more of our aunts and uncles and cousins, and having a very nice and exciting trip. On Saturday following the ballgame, there was lots of good eating and visiting. We did return to 'the city limits' late Saturday night, in order to be up and ready for early mass on Sunday. That night we stayed at a couple of dad's cousins' home and with his sister or brother and their families. Daddy and his cousin were so much alike that they could have been brothers, rather than being children of brothers. Our visit with them on Sunday gave us exposure to several experiences they had while growing up in the south. We made the return trip without any problems including a rest stop at maternal grandmother's home. Our excitement over the whole trip was the topic of conversation during the trip home. Knowing what I do now about driving etc., makes me feel all that much more proud of dear daddy during this outing. As it turned out, this trip was the only one that the family made enmasse, but there were other trips south that continued to surprise and teach me what strong yet gentle persons my parents were.

Upon returning home and to the paper route (which was managed by a very good family friend) I found that one of my regular customers and a real family friend died over the weekend.

This patient was a priest who our family had 'adopted' and took care of his business. It was quite a shock to me and difficult to understand since he did not appear outwardly to be as ill as he had been.

Having told about the trip south, and my drinking the 'White Only' water, I guess there should be mention of one other occurrence that is not forgotten as regards segregation. This is about my maternal grandmother's illness and subsequent death. She suffered a stroke while at work and was rushed to the hospital. The problem developed following her death, and that being none of her clothing and personal belongings were returned to the family at the time of her death. She became ill on a Friday and mother flew down to Alabama right away, she also had a son living in the same house with her, so he was at the hospital over the weekend most of the time prior to her death on the following Monday. Now to clarify the issue at hand, I must tell you that my uncle became ill once and required emergency treatment. My grandmother was at work and went immediately to the hospital, where she was informed she needed a certain amount of cash dollars before my uncle could be treated, irregardless of his condition. She had no other alternative but to catch a city bus to her home, and rush back to the hospital so he could be treated. From that experience, grandmother never traveled away from home with out a certain amount of cash on her person (and in her case in a pocket she had sewn inside of her corset). Well when she was admitted as an emergency patient, her employer paid the necessary fees for her treatment. There was a very fragile excuse given my mother and uncle at the time of her death, so someone had for themselves some extra pocket cash. When I arrived in town for the funeral and learned these details, I begged momma and my uncle to let me stay over an extra day to help resolve the situation (I was now a registered nurse and knew the proceedings were not handled correctly nor professionally), but momma and my uncle feared personal repercussions would happen once all the family left town. This racial incident had more effect on me and the family than any others that warrant being mentioned, not to say there were not more of greater magnitude, but once again I thank God for mom and dad and their approach in teaching us how to handle the situations we might be subjected to during our lifetime.

MY SIBLINGS

Seven of the nine of us children were born at home and of those births that I can recall (in retrospect of my medical knowledge or that of being a heavy sleeper), no matter how difficult the delivery, mom's humility and non-complaining manner will long be remembered.

There was a very dear friend of mother's that always appeared on the scene right after the arrival of a new baby, and she took over the housework and all other duties to keep the Smith household intact until mother was able to return to being the wonderful mom she always was, in other words when she could be up and around as usual. This lovely lady continued her close ties with our family for what seemed like forever. She and mom's friendship helped us children to learn all about loving, caring and sharing. From our child-like perspective of the friendship she was remembered for the delicious yellow birthday cakes she made from scratch using the infamous "Swans Down Cake Flour' (which recently I actually saw in a supermarket) for each one of us on our birthday for many years. I was 16 years old when this dear friend baked the last one for me. Her husband and daddy were naturally good friends also and they were musically connected, having played in a dance band together in the 40's. Daddy played both trumpet and trombone and he dawdled at the piano, while his friend mastered the BIG BASE FIDDLE. Incidentally, daddy was a self-taught musician for the most part. He always wanted some of us to pursue a musical career, but no one advanced beyond piano lessons in secondary grades and ballet lessons in the early (years – 3rd thru 6th grade) if that long. My son did show an interest in the drums during his junior high years, but music lost out to sports.

Although mom's friend wasn't needed following the birth of the last three children (the older girls were able to help with housework), she remained in close contact. As fate would have it, when we moved the next time it was discovered (by us children) that this friend and her husband lived one block away on the same street. I now know that they probably gave mom and dad some information regarding this particular house being for sale. Somehow I became a favorite of mom's friend and this allowed me to be her 'adopted little girl', thus letting me spend several nights at her home during the summer months when school was not in session.

By way of introduction here goes the real story (short and hopefully sweet) of my siblings: The first born a daughter, was destined for good things from her early school days. She completed elementary school in 7 years rather than the usual 8 years. This was accomplished without her missing a single day of classes. She continued to excel in high school at the one catholic school that granted admission to Negroes. She earned a scholarship to the local catholic college, which she attended for two years before cupid shot his arrow toward her and she got married and started her family of 13 children (10 living). The mother of necessity naturally required her to be a working mother, she continued as such between pregnancies as a government worker, and that of a teacher in the same parochial school, which she attended. Her college training and the fact she continued to pursue her degree(s) in education made her eligible to teach at this time prior to completing her college courses. She managed to juggle her already full schedule and after 25 years from her first college exposure she received her bachelor's degree in education, and also a master's degree with 30 hours plus. Her teaching career then turned to special education and she began working at The Boy's Correctional Institution where she remained until her retirement 21 years later. Following her retirement she continued working as a volunteer once or twice a week, and also was a regular substitute teacher in an inner city parochial school. Finally, mention is made of the terrific influence she is and has been to her grandchildren, and now works on influencing the great grandchildren. She has been widowed several years.

Child #2 another daughter is a Missionary Nun and like all the children her early exposure at various levels of employment at the hospital helped formulate the ideas for her career choices.

She wanted a nursing career and also had envisioned herself as a religious nun when she was very young, according to information from mother several years ago. Upon completion of high school, which was a different school than the one attended by her older sister, (because of the efforts of The Bishop, and the enactment of certain laws – a person could not be denied admission to an institution of learning because of race, creed or color). Believing that this 'law' was for all levels of education, an application was made for nurses training at the Catholic Hospital, which was denied, but for reasons other than the fact that Negro students were not being accepted at this time. Not to be denied the chances to further her education, classes were taken at Indiana University Downtown Extension for several semesters before the time arrived for a change in direction and at this point she was ready to join a religious order in preparation for her being a missionary nun, and subsequently her training as a Licensed Practical Nurse as well as becoming a Registered Nurse while studying in London, England. Her professional training also includes becoming a licensed midwife, a holder of a double bachelor's degree and to this she has added a master's degree and continues to keep abreast with various classes and seminars. The stories of her experiences while working abroad are never heard too often. Sister spent many, many years in East Africa and was there during some anxious times with previous dictators/ rulers of the area. Sister is a frequent speaker, and is currently working with The Office of Catholic Missions for the Archdiocese of Indiana and it gives her a chance to be involved with the school children, and also makes her a favorite 'Auntie' at the same time.

Child #3 is me, myself and I, so automatically the oldest boy was next in line.

Child #4 My brother was very athletically inclined, for this I can fully attest to from the number of times I had to bail him out of trouble by completing his paper route. This occurred because the ballgame(s) pick up style, in any of the sports had a stronger pull at his heart strings than the work to be done in the form of delivering his paper route. Things became much better for the family at the point he switched (dad orchestrated the change) to selling the morning papers in the hospital and he was not drawn away by the old ball games. His escapades of ball playing did pay off during his high school days, as he played football and basketball very well and was a member of championship teams more than once. All his sports activity was the start of my being a sports fanatic, rather than your average fan. While I was away at school, he met his future wife, and following their marriage and his joining the Air Force, he moved out of state. They had 3 children. My brother was a jet mechanic and it was while doing this job, he met his untimely death at the age of 20.

Child #5 is another girl. She fell heir to the evening paper route in the hospital when I entered nurses' training. Seemingly a medical career or one associated with hospital(s) did not appeal to her, and she sought employment elsewhere as her school days drew to an end. The phone company one place she applied for work) called her four days prior to her graduation day, with a job offer which she accepted and a place of employment she continued the next 35 ½ years. Her marriage of which three children were born did terminate in divorce, but my sister was strong and stood tall. She went back to school and acquired a degree in business (which resulted in her promotion to management positions) and she was able to fin for herself, and since her children were old enough to give support instead of being at a stage when they needed more than they could give. Her phone company retirement (actually downsizing) led her to volunteering at the elementary school she graduated from (the same school and church we could see from our front porch many years ago, but not able to attend) and that was the start of a second career. She became the school secretary and continues that job currently. She is a doting grandmother, and active in her parish church. She shares her home with our sister and brother who are members of religious congregations, and since the original family home does not exist any longer it gives both of them a 'home away from home'.

Child #6 was the baby girl for 11 years to be exact and has been known as 'the boss' all along. This name best fits her now more than ever since we are all adults with our own families. I am sure her 2 sons would also give the thumbs up to this fact of her being 'the boss'. Although she is retired and busier than ever, she was a very dynamic force working in and for the cause of mental health and it's many facets as a social worker. Through many trials and tribulations she returned to school and completed degrees (Bachelor and Masters) in social work. She and her husband enjoy fixing their home and entertaining the families at every chance or reason that can be designated as party time.

They have support and help from the two boys who were aptly named 'big' and 'stretch' by a cousin many years ago, because of their respective statures. This cousin is now a combination of both of them and played football at a Big 10 College.

Child #7 the second son, the lawyer, politician, sports buff, and Air Force veteran, keeps the memories of our growing up with his amusing and entertaining stories about the paper routes, and various jobs we all had very close at hand. He has done a marvelous job being the figurehead for the family especially since dad passed away. He and his wife have three grown children and the youngest, a recent graduate of a medical school is keeping pace with her older sister and brother both who are practicing attorneys. Although my brother's many jobs have required a lot of travel and quite often very demanding, he remains completely in touch with the family and on top of important matters for everyone. He and his wife now enjoy the fruits of having educated the three children, and look forward to the future free of tuition paying days.

Child #8 the third boy, contributed many a memorable moment to the family history by way of the paper route (which he naturally inherited) and his various neighborhood jobs and chores. He became a three sport all-star athlete in high school (the same one that his big brother attended and excelled in sports). Thus he had some real soul searching to contend with following his graduation because of his vocational aspirations versus accepting one of many scholarship offers he had received. He ultimately chose to pursue his religious vocation as did his sister. What a tremendous choice this turned out to be. His choice can be verified upon review of his accomplishments. Yet he remains a very humble person. The many assignments have found him as a secondary elementary teacher, a worker in homes for troubled boys, the personnel director for his congregation's Midwest Province, and the director and social worker for The Catholic Social Service Center in northern Indiana, which as a result of his dedication to this job, made him eligible for the honor of an outstanding citizen of the city. Just like his sister, child #7 he holds a masters degree in social work and is currently the guidance counselor in a high school in Illinois.

Child #9 The "bay-ay bee" (as only her husband can pronounce) arrived the summer between my junior and senior year in high school and she thereby bumped her older sister from the baby girl spot. She (rather they) managed to survive the usual sibling rivalry, she also became a person All Grown Up Dressed in White. Her nursing jobs include supervisor in local treatment center for drug and alcohol, medical nursing, psychiatric nursing and most recently working for the state in a nursing capacity. She has two unique children who currently keep all of us in touch with our childhoods and also keep us busy attending various sporting events, which they are either participating in or just have corralled the family into going and being there with them. Like his cousins before him her son(the Big 10 Player) has excelled in both basketball and football and as a freshman (the 1st in 25 years history of his high school) was awarded a varsity letter for football. Her daughter is active in and around the cheerleaders and very attentive to her brothers' games. It is often said that she is of such a personality that she could be subject of her own book and not just a small part of this offering of mine. Rest assured she shall be heard from like her brother as she is doing outstanding work academically and otherwise. NOTE: that from the beginning efforts of telling you about my siblings, a few moons have come and gone to the tune of years, and #9 siblings son continues his outstanding play and made it with his college team to play in 'The Rose Bowl 2000'.

The Siblings continue their winning ways, and of course are constantly giving me encouragement to complete my manuscript, so I am now much closer to being the author of "All Grown Up and Dressed In White".

PREPARATION FOR NURSING SCHOOL

Our family's connection with the hospital (dad's place of employment) was and will always be remembered. It can be referred to as our vault of happy memories. Many acts of kindness were extended to us throughout the years. There were for instance, the shopping trips for shoes, socks, and underwear that were so welcomed at the beginning of the school year and then again in the Spring around Easter. The Daughters of Charity made sure by such kind acts as these that Daddy's children were provided with important essential items, which his salary would not always stretch far enough to allow us to have. Believe me, the items were nothing extravagant, and we children knew the value of a dollar, making us much more appreciative.

As briefly mentioned earlier about the various areas in the hospital that some of us worked gave us a common ground meeting place when ready to go home. This common meeting place turned out to be The Main Kitchen. The nun in charge of this area for as long as I can remember was the dearest, kindest person I can recall having known. Not only did she give me inspiration but also encouragement in my aspirations. (As is mentioned further into my story, how some aspects of encouragement etc., were lacking). Sister made my 1st year in nursing more tolerable by keeping me supplied with the best C.A.R.E. Packages ever prepared and sent to a student. The Main Kitchen nun and her employees gave the biggest and best party to honor my leaving for school. A real treat and surprise was the beautiful and delicious cake, prepared by the head of the pastry area and it was in the shape of an open book of knowledge to help me become a good nurse.

Other bylines that make the hospital and the administrators so near and dear to our hearts include the establishment of the photo gallery at the present location with pictorial tributes to long time employees(which includes a photo of daddy). This inclusion of daddy's photo was done following a sort of protest by the nurses' alumnae association when the newly named streets surrounding the hospital did not include a street named for him. The picture compensated for the failure to honor his 41 ½ years of employment. Now circa the '90s the hospital has dedicated a video conference room to dad's memory at the hotel conference center across the street from the hospital.

With all these memories, and factors in mind and I was at the point of making plans for my career, it was ironic that I could not look forward to attending nursing school right where I had spent so much time. Because my sister had been refused admission to the school of nursing, I did not consider applying, and when the word of my choice of schools did surface, it caused a bit of a shockwave at the hospital. (Negroes were admitted the same year that I started in my training.)

At this point of my life (I was a junior in high school) and can remember mom's non complaining attitude and doing what comes naturally approach to life that was a powerful force in all of our lives'. We often dreamed of things which seemed impossible to achieve and maybe even put them aside as insurmountable, but momma could and would be that spark which rekindled us and made us keep on pushing toward the dream. Counselors and goals were but a couple of words in the vocabulary, and almost non-existent in my formative years. If I dared voice my dreams or thoughts of being a nurse, it was met with comments like "Are you sure that's what you want"? Or even statements like "that's hard work". Very seldom was there any form of positive comments (except from mom and dad and the nun in the main kitchen). However, I do recall one helpful assignment I was given in elementary school after I began talking about wanting to be a nurse. That assignment was being the runner for the school nurse, when she and the doctor made their visits to our school for immunizations and general check ups that we were afforded before the establishment of Public Health Clinics. Despite the negative aspects I met up with, I continued my pursuit of being a nurse. I did finally receive help regarding types of courses to take in high school and other helpful hints from one of the graduate registered nurses (an administrator in the school of nursing) who also happened to be one of my daily customers on the paper route. My own nosey demeanor while I worked various summer jobs proved to be very beneficial. One job in particular was an assignment in housekeeping department of the nurses' residence hall in the area of the classrooms. Common knowledge reveals that nurses attended classes year round during the times of the 3 year diploma programs. This one fact made it convenient for the aspiring nurse to listen in on some lectures outside the classrooms and gain more insight into the future. This in a long run was valuable.(The floors outside these classrooms probably would have passed the 'white glove' test several times during that summer). One of the instructors I listened to then, later on became one of my instructors some 4 years later. She was a very endearing and understanding person. Other summer jobs, which proved to be helpful during my nursing and professional working days, were as an aide in the radiology department transporting some patients, and assisting with some of the procedures. I also worked in admissions area and last but not least the dietary department.

I began my correspondence with other Catholic Hospitals located fairly close to home and was truly inspired when one school of nursing located about 35 miles away accepted my application and thus the intense actions were begun to complete the necessary requirements needed for the next year following my graduation from high school. This also made the chore of checking the mail a daily ritual. My high school senior year was upon me very soon and was history just as fast. The days began to pass quickly, and the time for my departure grew closer. There was only one 'dark' cloud which cast a shadow over me now and that was the letter informing me that my first year of nursing would be spent in the northern part of the state over 130 miles away instead of being located only 35 miles away.

PART II

NURSES TRAINING – A REALITY

Carrie (Ginny Girl) Kemp

THE ARRIVAL

Believe it or not, daybreak did finally arrive on September 2, 1952 despite the fact that one excited young lady spent a rather wakeful night hearing every sound that was audible in the city limits, and even heard a train whistle, which was not that close to her home. This perhaps was the second longest night in her life, the first being awake most of the night in pain from a severely sprained ankle. To the best of my recollections this was a Tuesday and my departing home for nurses' training was a brand new situation for the family. My two older sisters had done their college studying locally. Throughout all my excitement, sadness, and all the other emotions experienced this particular day, I can hardly remember the 3-4 hour drive to my home away from home for the next three years.

I recall our arrival was close to 12 noon, and there were 119 other families going thru the same process. Nursing school enrollments had dwindled to a new low in the year or two prior to my application. However, increased recruiting, and in the case of my alma mater, the reduction of tuition resulted in the number of applicants accepted for this class to be 120 girls/women. The lower tuition was a tremendous help, since I was helping with my fees, books, etc., from paper route savings. These savings were in a real bank. (Not the mustard jar type spoken of earlier in my story). This particular bank is the same one that my husband and I still use some 40 years hence, just having gone thru several reorganization periods, and name changes by deleting some words and adding others to its name.

Although there were 7 new 'probie nurses' in the group, from my same home town and the same high school the old nemesis known as home sickness struck real quick. Now I ask, what can be said about being homesick that isn't experienced universally in late August or early September? 'Ma Bell' has survived many a fictitious flood (in the phone booths) from the tears shed by the likes of myself when the infamous phone calls from home were made or received.

GETTING DOWN TO BUSINESS

With the number of students being 120 in the freshman class, it required us to be divided into two groups. Using the old reliable alphabetical way, I ended up in the second group since my last name began with an S. This only meant still longer time before uniforms and patient contact were to be a reality. There's good in all situations, I feel certain, as I look back on my situation, that had I not been assigned those 1st five months for intense studies, I might not have come out of the 'sea' of learning without drowning. On one occasion, our instructor told us the classes were like a deep sea, and we could sink or swim. With that bit of advice, I began a gurgling noise in the back of the classroom, to the amusement of fellow classmates. As we left the classroom that day, the instructor beckoned me toward her office. Well rest assured, there were few if not any other times I let my mouth get me in trouble after that episode. I guess it was more than a few times, but nothing really serious. This particular instructor was my biggest influence and an all around friend. She was beyond words when you try to describe her, and she had overcome several obstacles to reach her current plateau. Her greatest obstacle was having been a polio patient and confined to an iron lung at one time. Whenever the going got rough or things were not going as she maybe wanted, she would pull out her top desk drawer and reveal a photo of herself when she was dependent on the iron lung. This photo told a story without words, and naturally became an incentive for those of us who had fewer problems and less obstacles than depicted by the picture.

Speaking of obstacles, I had my biggest test of fortitude confront me during this first year. The Anatomy and

Physiology Laboratory was located about 2-3 miles from our residence on one of the college campuses. St. Mary's College was across from the one and only Notre Dame University. What could and should have been an exciting twice weekly trip to the lab classes was dampened by the fact that "Odie" my lab animal was a cat. (The cats' full name was Odiferious). Now let it be known that since very early in my life cats or any of the feline category were not a favorite of mine or any of us children. I mean no harm to those who do care for cats, but to each his own. Well, I may have been the first to use the rubber gloves (big thick ones as used for housecleaning chores nowadays) in this particular lab classroom, but believe me it was my only means of survival. I guess the instructor had some pity for my feelings, and I did manage a passing grade for the combined portion of Anatomy and Physiology lab classes.

February (the long awaited time for our group to don our uniform) did not take as long as expected to roll around and signal that the 2nd half of the class of '55 was to begin clinical training with uniforms, patient contact and the whole ball of wax. Our uniforms were different than the ones I described as being worn by the student nurses at the hospital back home. The uniform was a one-piece all white heavy cotton dress, with the school name and emblem on the left breast pocket. Freshman students were clearly identifiable with their probation 'probie' caps, which in a word left something to be desired, but also gave much more meaning to the capping ceremony held at the end of nine months of study and clinical practice. Class members often referred to those nine months as having our first child without conception.

It is often said, "that to be successful, one must be able to wear many hats," and my comments to that are to be successful as a nurse one hat is enough, as long as it is worn by someone with patience for the patients, lots of understanding, and most of all the ability to disperse a big dose of TLC.

I would truly be remiss if I did not mention a few words surrounding the social activities of the 3years of nursing school days. The ND students along with ST. Mary's College students and of course the Holy Cross Central School of Nursing students participated in frequent 'mixers', and these were always a lot of fun. If by chance you were unfamiliar with a mixer, it is when a group of students get together for fun and quite a few lasting friendships were developed as the result of these get-togethers. However, I was introduced to one young man by his sister who happened to work at the hospital where I was to do my clinical studies in the first year . We began dating regularly and the Saturday night dates to the movie with a stopover at the favorite college age hangout known as 'The Kwepie Doll'. This unusual restaurant specialized in serving the ever popular hamburger/cheeseburger with fries and a beverage at the affordable price for these days and times and before the advent of McDonald's fast food eating places. With a good movie and meal taken care of, the walk back to the dormitory (weather permitting) was always enjoyed. Our dating and friendship lasted for about 1 ½ to 2years, but distance soon drove a wedge in that romance and we parted amicably shortly after the summer of 1954.

Another social event that is still recalled during the 1st year of training was the Friday evenings enjoyed with a classmate and her family. There were 6 or 7 of us rescued from the halls of the dorm and the meatless suppers that were offered in the cafeteria. Talk about a source of aggravation and being in need of culinary bypass is a kind comment used when describing the menus on some Friday evenings in the hospital cafeteria. Of course this was during the days and times of mandatory meatless Friday meals. I suppose my own mother's home cooked Friday meals had spoiled our family. The menu was something like salmon croquets, vegetables, macaroni and cheese with hot homemade (from scratch) rolls that would melt in your mouth. Back to the schooldays' Friday meals, my classmates' parents were both in on the royal treatment, dad came to the dorm to pick us up, irregardless of the weather which in that particular area of the state was and still continues to be horrible in the winter, and mom always had something very deliciously prepared waiting for us. After a fun filled, and food filled evening dear dad took us back to the dormitory. This classmate and I are still in frequent contact, and it is so much fun to recall these episodes that occurred while in school.

In May 1953, I found myself armed with the school cap, (signifying the successful completion of clinical and academic studies to this point) and ready to take on the world of a second year (a junior) nursing student. There were beds to make, baths to be given, flowers to be tended to, fresh water to drink that had to be passed out, meal trays served, patients fed and also cleaning the units following a patient's dismissal. Several of these assignments or duties were delegated to other classifications of employees throughout my days of employment, but I somehow feel that having been there and done that, made it much easier to maintain calm and a spirit of working together much simpler.

It was not very long before our overnight transformation increased our responsibilities and job assignments included passing medications, giving enemas performing other tedious and advanced duties. Oh by the way, classes continued and they were more advanced and becoming more complicated resulting in a very full schedule. You might recall at the beginning of this journey I mentioned that my correspondence was with a school located only 35 miles from home, well I was ready for that location at this point of training. Probably within the month following our capping ceremony, and increased responsibilities, the sweet music to ones ears of moving on to the other affiliated hospitals with connections to the present location and hospital operated by the same type of nuns was indeed a reality. Incidentally, of the 120 students that started in the class, around 95 of us persevered to reach this point. Moving closer to home was just fine, but it also meant saying goodbye (until graduation) to some of my very dear friends and classmates. Classes held year round was a new twist for some, (but recalling my summer jobs held as a teenager made the transition an easy one for me). Then I also figured it was time to put in perspective a quotation I kept uppermost in my mind which to coin the phrase "When Your Eye Is On The Prize" all things are possible. In retrospect, the days of nurses' training seemed to move at a slow pace, but now they are remembered with fondness and leads me to say "Time flies when you are having fun".

Year #2 found us in a different type dormitory, the nurses' quarters, or whatever was a delightful place known as Raphael Hall. From the outside it gave the appearance of a large colonial style home in the south, the large porches with rocking chairs, on both the first and second levels and the large columns seen in and around the front entrance. At any rate, it housed probably 60 of us students and the live-in housemother affectionately known as 'Mom B' who shared her first floor quarters with a beautiful collie named Lady. Oh what I or any number of the classmates would give for one of those 45 minute class breaks and a good competitive game of contract bridge. It was a real scramble for one of the three card tables available for the in between classes and clinical duties free time. The soaps (non existent on TV) were not of interest to our class, but the card game did take a back seat at prime time television watching when it was time for different variety type shows, such as Arthur Godfrey and Liberace and when certain artist made special appearances on these shows. One real favorite of the Raphael Hall gang, was 'hizzoner' Julius LaRosa was making a visit to Arthur Godfrey's show. This brings to mind one of our more memorable group outings, (I often wonder how we pulled it off especially with automobile ownership being a real rarity), we traveled 30 miles or thereabout northeast of our location to one of the colleges for a concert featuring Julius LaRosa. What with our screams, swoons and general noise in the audience, we had the spotlight on us as much as the performers on stage. Just the same it was great fun and enjoyment by everyone. By the way, just in case anyone thought different, study hours were maintained and TV was not allowed during certain hours, so it was a real treat to see these certain shows.

Junior year (the 2nd year) of nurses training was rapidly passing by and the classes with clinical practice was all coming together rather nicely. My grades were being maintained. At this point I recalled rather vividly the morning three years hence, that I ventured from home to take the pre-entrance exam for possible admission to a nursing school. My performance on this exam was deemed not very good, but because Of high personal recommendations, and I suppose my determination, I was informed that I would be accepted on the condition that I kept a 'C' average throughout my studies. Well the maintaining the necessary average was not the problem, with one particular class, namely Pathology. This class in itself was a difficult one to grasp by the handle, (this fact was seconded by the scholars of our class) but insult was added to injury by the professor, he was so wrapped up in his field of medicine he was unable to impart his knowledge to us as students, thereby causing many of the class members to become concerned about a passing grade. I passed the course as most of my fellow classmates, and it was smooth sailing grade wise from then until the finish line was crossed. The clinical settings were sometimes a cause to hit a stumbling block or two, this developed by way of the head nurses, who I think were put on this earth to place the fear of God in us students, thus forgetting that they had passed this same path not too very long ago. (It was at this point I vowed to be a compassionate person if and when I reached supervisory status, which I feel I did accomplish, but maybe not in everyone's eyesight.) Even thou I had many, many bad days, I admit I was never at the point of wanting to quit, thus I tried to remain focused on being grown up and dressed in white.

It seemed that 'free' time always presented a new adventure, and since several of us were high school classmates and long time friends, adventures became the rule rather than the exception. I recall one trip to the state park for horseback riding, and what followed that particular adventure. Some of us had already completed our rotation thru the emergency room and knew a few angles of the workings in the department, we were also aware of the one classmate who was currently on duty this particular evening was most uncomfortable in that position. Well, this being a small town 'real' emergencies were few and far between and so we cased the area, making sure all was quiet on the home front, which did appear to be just that, so we proceeded to the next step that of staging a fake injury to one of us and go rushing into the emergency room to play a joke on our unknowing classmate. It worked real well, what with the superb acting of some of the group. Thankfully we did not get into much trouble, but I truly received payback for being a part of the whole plan to a certain extent. By the way, the fake injury was a compound fracture of one girl's leg after she fell off the horse. After restoring calm in the area, and settling our classmate so she could remain on duty for the remainder of her shift, we proceeded to the dorm, and of course the news of the prank spread like wildfire. After finishing a shower and change of clothes to begin studying, I developed an increased difficulty seeing out of one of my eyes and of course the condition warranted emergency treatment. The cause was never clearly determined, unless it was an allergic reaction of some type acquired while on the horse-back riding trail. Of course the same student was still on duty and she 'innocently' relayed the early evening events of our trick to the doctor who treated me for my eye problem. He thought it was very amusing, but also bandaged my eye with an unusually large dressing with explicit instructions that I could work as scheduled, but must leave the bandage in place for 48 hours. The eventual joke was literally and figuratively on me. Recalling this event and other 'pranks' that occurred when I was in school, made it easy to understand that my whereabouts was determined or established before looking elsewhere for the culprit(s) when mischievous acts were committed.

Aside from being a prankster, nursing duties and responsibilities continued to become more advanced, mostly involving assignments to work an evening shift, with charge nurse duties. Our class members also began to travel around 'off campus' for classes and clinical experiences in pediatrics, public health, and psychiatric nursing. These travels were known as affiliation assignments. My travel days, thankfully, were all assigned one right after the other and started in December 1954 thereby ending the week of graduation, which was scheduled for August 1955.

The stories and experiences of this period may well be enough for a complete book some time in the future, but I am only touching lightly on them now. Psychiatric training was the first stop, (this meant a return to the northern part of the state) far away from home again, but somewhat compensated by the newness of the facility and the nurses' living accommodations. Our rooms, all private ones, and the off time was a bit more liberal, of course we were fast approaching adulthood, which made us more responsible. Not to mention we were almost located in 'no mans' land about 25-30 miles from civilization so the trouble one could get into, required a means of transportation. The lights out at 10 P.M. in the nurses' residence on Monday thru Thursday was par for the course and Friday, Saturday, and Sunday were get away nights. Had I not been embarking on the final eight months of training I might have been heading home, following the rude awakening with the introduction to psychiatry. This intro was on the acutely ill female unit. Enough said on this subject. The 12 weeks spent on this affiliation opened my eyes as it was intended to do and made me thankful for many, many things. The next assignment (8 weeks of study) dealt with rural health nursing. The location was out of state. The assignments for accompanying the public health nurses were at an all time low, thereby we had a lot of extra work time in the hospital under the direction of nuns that had been located at our other home hospitals. During this time I experienced some 'private duty' nursing which proved to be unglamorous to me. The different times I worked as a private duty nurse, the patient was in my estimation in less need of private duty care than the patients I was use to caring for on a daily basis. What I mean by this statement is the procedure for one patient is now done in the doctor's office, and under local anesthesia, or at least as an outpatient. The money ($1.00 per hour) was very nice for pocket change, but still I was certain from then on, this aspect of nursing would not be one of my choices. It was now spring and it made trips to the local ice cream parlor and listening to the jukebox a frequent and favorite pastime for all of us. Thankfully, now some 40 years plus many of us still get together for old times sake, and reminiscence about these days of oldies but goodies. Time continued to march forward, and the final affiliation was upon us, and following a truly hysterical weekend trip back home, literally and figuratively, courtesy of one classmate's boyfriend. The car was filled beyond capacity with both passengers and luggage, but the grace of God spared us any problems and thus a safe arrival home. After a weekend visit truly at home with mom and dad, it was off to the west side of town to report for pediatric nursing at the local children's hospital. Working in the hometown was not what I guess was expected. The rules being the same for all students, local and otherwise, meant everyone in the living quarters and ready for study by 7:30

P.M. unless you were on duty. This was each weekday night and if you may have realized by now that this was summer time. There might be another book or something titled 'The Summer of 1955' in the future. But all efforts are being consumed on this manuscript. Midnight passes were granted or allowed on the weekends (if not scheduled to work). Naturally, yours truly encountered one of the penalties for missing a curfew. I had been to a formal dance, unfortunately, my dates car was blocked in the parking area, creating the situations of my being late returning to the dormitory. The subsequent punishment was more humiliating than unbearable. I am certain that aside from all else, these 12 weeks of study and clinical practice will leave indelible marks with me, because of the fact our time spent at the children's hospital was pre-Salk Vaccine polio period. Many of the children were being treated for polio and it's complications. There were many other childhood illnesses requiring intense nursing care, and it was also a period before broad spectrum antibiotics came into being. In retrospect, the overall situations which were encountered made me more aware, and created a sense of appreciation for wellness. Following one rather vigorous week of studies, and duty hours including split shifts, long evening tours of duty, my 'wellness' fell by the wayside. The work load one particular evening shift 3-11 P.M. caused me to work an extra 2 hours (not by choice) in order to complete my work. My co-worker became ill on duty and the other two persons on duty were dental students that worked extra and not allowed to work on the general ward, or work overtime. Following my 1:00 A.M. departure, only to sleep fast and return on duty at 8A.M. I succumbed to an acute bronchial asthma attack (new diagnosis) and was in the infirmary for one week. This was my second time of being a patient, and leading me to the thought I still continue to live by. "It is better to give than receive when it comes to medicine." It has also been said you are not a good nurse until you have been a patient. Believe me, if the decision was left to me, I make and second the motion and cast the deciding vote for the fact that I am a good nurse. This title was given to me on one of my jobs following graduation when I worked the evening shift, the patients called me 'the goodnight nurse' and the good night nurse. This hospitalization was my second experience of being a patient while I was a nursing student. The other one was during the Christmas Holidays in 1953, I spent several days for recurrent symptoms and pain in the lower right quadrant of my abdomen. One thing that was determined I was not pregnant (no recent stars had appeared in the eastern sky denoting immaculate conceptions) and appendicitis was ruled out. The culprit presented itself some eight years later, 1961 vintage, when a large ovarian cyst(retro-positioned in the pelvis) with obvious signs of degeneration from longevity was removed. The 7 days spent for the asthma treatment and this hospitalization amounted to the maximum 'sick' days allotted students, and thus when graduation day arrived, I was a free person. Some classmates had to return for 1 or two days make up work.

The prize was now in sight, and graduation day was a reality, 3 cheers for the fact I was getting ready to work as a graduate at the hospital where my early aspirations began some twelve years ago. The mere fact that we were about to graduate, gave us (the prankster classmates and myself) the opportunity to pull some kind of a prank, as our group became noted for performing. Well, our last shot was having breakfast in the canteen, rather than the usual cafeteria and blasting the jukebox (6:00 A.M.) and just making havoc that hour of the morning. Needless to say for the hospital it was farewell and good riddance to our group of affiliates.

GRADUATION

Whether it be from Daycare to Kindergarten – Kindergarten Days to 1st grade or anywhere along life's chain, which denotes successful completion, and that progress has been attained, the graduate is ready to take on the world or be devoured by the great unknown. Graduation is the pinnacle.

As is recalled throughout this story, my adventures into being grown up had involved travel time along with studies (mostly studies), and the travel time scheduled for late in the summer of 1955 turned out to be the winning production.

It is funny how this 3 1/2-hour drive back to the northern part of the state was so very different from the trip made three years ago.

Having completed my days as a student nurse right at home (meaning in my hometown) made plans for the itinerary(weekend of graduation activities) much simpler to plan and dear daddy was allowing me to drive myself back to the location of graduation. I took off accompanied by 2 classmates and we managed to arrive safely and on time. Room assignments were secured and besides all the meeting and greeting of classmates not seen over the past years since our capping ceremonies there was a lot to get done. Visiting friends and just checking out the city was next in line for the senior nurses about to graduate. As might be expected, there were still rules to be adhered to such as curfew, quiet times, and lights out times. Well time caught up with us and we were literally locked out. Thank goodness for one industrious student who was found to be up late "cracking" the books. Yes, we were finally able to get her attention. Her room was on an upper level. We gained entrance thru the fire door. This grand entry was probably witnessed by more folks than we know, but nothing was said to us, so the 'curfew busters' dismissed the issue. (Out of sight Out of mind) except on the way down the elevator sometime over the weekend a young lady pleaded with us not to tell that she was the one that let us in the fire door. Well you can imagine how stupid we would have been to think of reporting anyone or any such incident. This was only the beginning of a wild weekend and yours truly with some classmates added fuel to the fire by ingesting some "sample" medicine that was legally obtained from the pharmaceutical representative (in days gone by they were the drug detail man). Without a detailed technicolor version of this portion of the weekend let it be known that a hard lesson was learned when the "bottom" fell out on Sunday after mass and before the actual graduation ceremony. My family, who had now arrived in town, was quite concerned, but I managed to pull it all together for graduation, and the drive home of the nurse now "All Grown Up and Dressed In White"

Following the arrival by mail of my school pin, which was not legally awarded until the third anniversary of the date of entering school, made my graduation complete by the end of the week, which began with the actual graduation ceremony.

The transition from dormitory vs. home living was not a problem and having accomplished this matter and being in a good comfort zone, I sought employment at the hospital (walking distance from home) where my journey originated with the paper route and all the helpful and valuable summer jobs I worked while in pursuit of this dream.

There were several areas/divisions of nursing that I had envisioned myself to work when I did graduate. These areas were Men's Medical Unit, A Doctor's Office and work of some type in The Veteran's Hospital. As fate would have it, I experienced working in all three situations, as well obstetrical nursing (labor, delivery and postpartum care) both in the hospital, and as physician's nurse in his office. I also worked in research and oncology before my final curtain was dropped.

The first job as a graduate nurse was on a men's medical unit (heart attacks, strokes, and ulcers were the main menu. This was prior to intensive care, and other specialty units that are the rule for critically ill patients in the hospital today. My best recollection of the assignments called for the new graduates giving bedside care, baths and bedside treatments and other times being the medicine nurse. The particular job of being the medication nurse on this medical unit was probably the biggest factor which assisted in my aging process early on in life. There was such emphasis made about the blood thinners needing to be given daily at 2 P.M. sharp (this meant that 50% of all the patients on the unit were in this category) and made it difficult to deliver an order as such to over 15 patients. Dosage for each patient was contingent on the results of his A.M. blood work (prothrombin time). Once the physician was notified of the test results, it was a matter of praying that the pharmacy was on the ball, and able to dispense the medicine to the nursing unit in a timely manner, and allowing the medicine nurse to accomplish this feat. Well, as one might expect, there were enumerable times that I sat straight up in bed (dreaming) better yet having nightmares, that a dose was missed or not charted or that something went wrong on a particular day. (You can glean a little bit of how my aging process began so early in life.) The other factor allowing the assigned medicine nurse to experience 'never a dull moment(s)' type of day on an average eight-hour shift was the ever so popular S-T-R-I-C-T SIPPY DIET (1950's vintage) for acute ulcer patients.

This diet(?) consisted of antacids and half and half milk given alternately every waking hour, which was in essence from 6A.M. until 10 P.M. Enough said for these duties. Despite the fact I had kept busy and as unbelievable as it sounds the new graduate aside from occasional review in preparation for upcoming state board exams, she was restless for classes and so three months later was enrolled as an undergraduate to further her knowledge in the nursing field. Incidentally, the first attempt at state board exams was unsuccessful, which was not really a surprise, since after two days of exams, I knew that my performance on the final test of the second day was not up to par, with the distractions caused by a squeaking door used by those who finished ahead of the two hour time limit. The second attempt the following spring was rewarded with full licenses and credentials as a registered nurse.

Under graduate classes were scheduled twice a week initially concentrating on bachelor's degree in nursing, which was not my real desire, because it seemed that advanced studies beyond the three year diploma program groomed individuals for supervisory positions or as clinical instructors. My first and last love was hands on nursing at the bedside. Fifteen months after graduation, and employment circumstances more or less forced me to make a request for a change of departments, and my request was that I not be assigned to an orthopedic unit, because I had suffered some back problems (requiring treatment) and orthopedic patients generally required lots of lifting and positioning. Well I not only was transferred to the orthopedic department, I represented the first day shift nurse to be assigned to some now considered very weird working hours, for instance, 9 to 5; 10 to 6; 11 A.M. to 7 P.M. few if any actual 7-3:30 shifts. This schedule created a problem with my evening classes and low man on the totem pole never gets a break. It was quite evident that my request for the new assignment with stipulations regarding no orthopedics, and my failure to pass board exams on the first try, all added up to the punishment. I also was known to stand my ground in various situations in the work area regarding what I considered good nursing care. (These feelings I carried into my retirement). To this very day, I have not changed my stance.

Well exploration of possible new places of employment began to surface, and of course hours, transportation etc., needed to be considered. Once these were worked out, in June 1957 I embarked on a career at the Veteran's Hospital.

POSTGRADUATE DEGREE

(A.K.A. MRS. DEGREE)

Employment at The Veteran's Hospital proved to be quite a factor in my future. Oh yes, the pay scale was very nice, but the body paid dearly. Once new employees (nurses especially) completed the standard 4 week orientation and they did not have plans to work a permanent evening or night shift with hours of 3:30 P.M. to 12 midnight or 12 midnight to 8:00 A.M. it was not unusual to work all three shifts within a seven day period and not work any overtime. My assignment was to the area that housed veterans with long term illnesses and in that category were tuberculosis patients, histoplasmosis patients, other upper respiratory infections, diagnosis undetermined at admission. Not only were there many interesting case histories, but it was also a time that new approaches were being investigated and new developments were being used for treatments of these patients. This knowledge was very helpful and made the work more interesting.

Two months into my employment at V.A. Hospital several changes took place. First of all I need to mention that a dear friend and neighbor gave me fair warning not to go and snatch a husband from the 'poor' sick veterans. Believe me husband hunting was far displaced (I thought) from my mind at this point, because two relationships since graduation had not materialized into anything serious. (Note* My friend and neighbor did end up directing and overseeing my wedding eleven months later.) I really wanted to merely get on with my professional duties and continue my learning process. As for the learning it became more difficult to attend classes in pursuit of a bachelor's degree, and was naturally put on hold due to the new work schedule mentioned earlier in this story. Crazy work schedules and all associated with this period did not seem to deter a certain person's aspirations, as it turned out not too long after my two months on the job I was tapped as being his future wife. (He was very much assured of himself.) My head nurse informed me of the fact that a certain patient was 'love struck' and he wanted very much to get to know me better.

My then future husband was close to being discharged and he was convinced of the fact that I was part of his future, he needed to square some things out in speedy fashion. Incidentally his hometown was about 110 miles away. At this point in his treatment he was allowed unlimited weekend passes, so a dinner date was requested and the wheels of our future began turning in rapid fashion.

Labor Day was upon us and I fortunately was already scheduled to have the holiday weekend off duty, so when the invitation to visit his hometown of Louisville, KY to meet his family was extended, I accepted after a few wrinkles were ironed out. The biggest hurdle was that of not owning transportation. Alas! Friends and co-workers came to the rescue and all signals were go from that point. A very enjoyable visit was experienced and some forty plus years later I feel that I passed 'the family inspection' with flying colors.

One month following discharge (MHB) meaning maximum hospital benefit my future husband returned to Indianapolis, armed with determination, fortitude, strong nerves and oh yes a diamond ring. (One of his sisters refers to his actions and intent when she tells the story of how he confided in her about his feelings and how he was off shopping (not window shopping) frequently and she knew he was quite serious with a request from him for help in establishing credit with a local jewelry store.) He naturally required a co-signer because he had not been able to work since discharge from the service. All aspects of this part of the story ended positively. Meanwhile back on my home front I was surprised, but did accept the proposal with the understanding that several loose ends needed to be tied before a date for a wedding could be set. All kinds of changes were to take place during the upcoming year, with the wedding being the most important. The matter of relocating out of state so that my husband to be could continue his education and prepare for a career in tailoring which would lead to his ownership of a business upon graduation and finally being a vocational teacher until his retirement.

Most nursing jobs at this time offered the 'luxury' of being off every other weekend, so the route between our homes became very well traveled, both by automobile and Greyhound Bus. My fiancé purchased his first car shortly after being released from the hospital and it remained our primary transportation for about 3 years.

It is a known fact that most modern day marriages (1950's vintage) did not require a dowry as such, but thanks to mom and her good cooking, I had to have the knowledge and know how of the preparation of two food items to take into my marriage. The two special items were homemade rolls, and lemon meringue pie made from scratch. Mom always had these two foods on the menu whenever the trip was made north to Indianapolis. She even went so far as to send him home on Sunday with another pie. Thus the dowry I took into my marriage. Thank God for the Pillsbury Doughboy for the piecrusts, and I still do very well with the rolls, and also appreciate the fact the taste buds for sweets are now diminished and that these (pies and rolls) cause too many pounds that are more difficult to shed, have cut the frequency of preparing them.

THE WEDDING

Following contacts made with the church in anticipation of the big day, and other inquiries having been made, the groom to be completed instructions and was baptized into the catholic faith. Having then set a date (May 17th), the green light began to burn constantly with all the plans needing to be done for a successful and beautiful wedding that we were blessed with, weather wise and all other aspects. It seemed certain that the phrase "Time Flies When You Are Having Fun" is a true fact. For the most part, what with several showers, and mom and dad hosting the rehearsal dinner at home I could not complain. Amidst all these activities we were able to find a furnished apartment that would be just what we needed, since our move to Western Kentucky would take place mid-August.

The wedding day, mass, breakfast and the reception all were the best. However, one small cloud hung over the day and that was the fact that the baby girl all of one month from being 7years old, was to have been my flower girl, and no thanks to a bout of chicken pox, followed very close with the measles made the end result a very weak flower girl and a disappointed bride-to-be. My dear brothers arranged it so she did not miss the entire celebration. They purposely lagged behind the family, when we left for the reception, to get her dressed in her wedding attire (actually her First Communion Dress), which had been worn 3 weeks earlier. They then bodily carried her into the reception for a brief visit and then back home she was taken. My nephew, already scheduled to be the ring bearer, was joined by his sister as the flower girl.

Wedding, honeymoon trip, return to work, and getting accustomed to a new name, all consumed so much time and energy that the moving time arrived sooner than we imagined. (We took a trip in June to seek information regarding housing and employment for myself. Both a place to live and prospects of a job were secured on this trip). The nursing supervisor that interviewed me asked if I had my uniform with me, and could I start working sooner than mid-August, maybe like the next week? This was exciting and reassuring news to a point, but with all situations there are always snags which prevent a smooth transition.

Moving day in August arrived and not too surprising was the fact that mother was conspicuously absent. Although three other siblings had left the nest (my oldest sister was married but still in town, next oldest sister was now in the convent as a missionary nun, and the brother (now deceased) had been away in the service), she did not want to be around for this moving day, so she conveniently planned her annual visit with her mother.

Having lived in a furnished apartment up until this time, all our earthly belongings could and would be moved via 'the almighty' 1956 Mercury. We packed the car to the gills. Although our immediate plans called for similar living arrangements, we needed to take several items which could and would be used once we were able to move into a place of our own. (We did find a rental house within the year.) All in all these items included clothing, utensils, and other wedding gifts which would be used immediately. Other gifts and duplicate ones were stored in the attic of mom and dad's home. The trip and the big move (7 hour trip) was made safely and the only casualty was a hole in the car's muffler discovered upon arrival at our destination. My husband feels that the hole in the muffler was caused by the overload of our belongings. The next move was done with professional help.

Earlier I made reference to the fact that there were snags encountered to prevent a smooth changeover and even though this was 1958, most of the problems revolved around segregation. (Once again a hearty thanks to my parents for the proper upbringing). The trip in June was the real eye opener to what we might be confronted with when we moved. Having discussed our plans of relocation with several of the nurses(co-workers) they all assured me that a job would be no problem. Well when we did arrive in the town of Paducah in the western part of the state, and made inquiries as to the location of the hospital, which I was told advertised and recruited R.N.'s each and every month, we were informed very politely that the hospital down on the river and on 'the other side of the railroad tracks' was where I needed to go for a job. The reason being, was no 'Colored' nurses worked at the hospital that I had read about in all the nursing journals. We changed our directions and found the hospital where I could work as well as the supervisor that wanted me to start work sooner and was spoken of earlier. At this point of arrival late August there was an opening on the OB-Gyn unit, which entailed working all areas, namely labor, delivery, newborn nursery and postoperative patients having had gynecological surgery. I was hired in for the salary of $2900.00 per year and as fate would have it, I thought it better not to be concerned with the difference in pay for 'Colored' R.N.'s versus other R.N's and just ride out the tide. I mainly wanted to work to supplement my husband's disability benefit and government school expense checks. Some causes I endured, and others caused me to explode as time would tell. I did remain employed at the same location for almost two years. My husband's courses at the Technical Vocational School covered a 2 year period.

DEALING WITH CHANGE

Segregation and separation continued to rear their ugly heads, but despite it all, survival won out. A few of the facts which made it difficult to survive so to speak dealt with treatment of 'Colored Patients', especially the obstetrical patients following their delivery. Once the patient was admitted and delivered, she was transferred to the 1st floor on the very far end (no exits visible) for postpartum care and the babies were put in their nursery, which was a room with less dimensions than 6ft x 9ft, with a sink and no windows. For the most part, the newborns were left unattended and unobserved until it was the time for feeding. The nurse (not always a registered nurse) was in charge of all the colored patients with a variety of illnesses, the newborns and also on standby for helping in the emergency room, which was located on the other end of the long corridor from the newborn nursery. The capacity for the unit was in the range of 36-40 patients. The mere knowledge of these facts caused a change of my plans.

By now September was here and classes got under way for my husband without any real hitches, and life in the new town seemed to become routine for us and we were a happy twosome, when the symptoms of early pregnancy sent me a stark message. I immediately informed the staff and my physician that I would be instituting a new concept of postpartum care for them and the hospital and it would be the lying in concept, that of the baby being in the room with it's mother following delivery. There could have been problems since the colored patients ward only had one private room, and a private room was the ideal set-up for this concept. The pregnancy did continue relatively well, but premature labor at 26 weeks resulted in delivery and my premature daughter didn't survive.

Some other absurd experiences dealt with the 4 green top tables designated for the colored employees to use while eating at lunch time. There were a grand total of 16 seats, a number much less than the total number of colored employees, so not much time was allotted them to sit down and eat. There was also the matter of 2 different employee Christmas Parties. The White employees were treated to a dinner dance party in the Grand Ballroom of the downtown hotel, while the Colored employees were 'granted' the use of the whole cafeteria. Needless to say, since I was very vocal about this in telling the powers that be, if we work together we can party together, I did not participate either of the 2 years that I spent in the area over Christmas. I am sure some of these incidents almost come under heading of fictional horror stories, but they are very real. The summer of 1959 two local girls home for the summer (one white and one colored) applied for summer work, they were both nursing students from different schools, but at the same

112

level of training and were hired, the white student was hired as a nursing student and allowed to wear her school cap, while the colored student was hired as a nurses aide and not allowed to wear her school cap. The real topper of my experiences was the fact that the hospital which I initially thought I would be working was so involved with segregation matters that if one of the colored employees was injured or became ill while on duty, they were transported by ambulance to the other hospital for treatment or admission. Believe me, I made sure that my former co-workers back home were aware of this and what a source of amusement for all of us whenever I was home on a visit. I was disappointed that the minorities were so use to this type treatment and did not speak up for their rights, nor did anyone act on their behalf. I mostly knew that this was a time in history that a lot of this type of treatment was deemed unlawful if challenged. Several individuals were saddened by the fact that after two years I would definitely be moving back to Indiana. They felt I could have made an impact in the community, but it apparently was not in the cards for me at this particular time in my life. Just for a moment I feel I need to relate one other story surrounding my first pregnancy, and that was not having mother come to town and help me during my recovery time. When I finally found out why she did not come as promised, it turned out she had fallen and injured her ankle rather severely, and traveling was not an option. Just about time for me to return to work (six weeks off duty was the norm, unlike today's rule of thumb deliver in the morning and go to work the next day) daddy was hospitalized and had surgery, so I did make a trip home. His recuperation was uneventful. The only sour note upon return to work was the fact that my first delivery which I encountered produced a beautiful stillborn infant. It caused me some problems, but my faith and support system (co-workers) sustained me.

RETURN TO INDY

Time was marching on and that included my husband's completion of his classes and his graduation drawing nearer. We had over the past year and one half established many new good friendships, but we were still anxious to move forward with plans for return to Indianapolis. During this time 1 ½ year period, we had moved into a house. The owner had been widowed, but she planned to move in with a relative out of town, so when we rented from her, some of the furnishings were left and we eventually purchased those items from her. During the spring break of 1960 we made a trip back to Indianapolis and another search for living quarters was underway and proved to be a successful search during this visit. The only drawback to speak of was, if we wanted this particular house (1/2 a double) we would have

115

to take possession in 30 days. The owners felt it not advisable to leave the house empty until July. It was decided that I would return to Indianapolis within the next 30 days, a move which was carried out. Upon our return to Kentucky for my husband to complete school, we found every free moment consumed with preparation to complete the move. Goodbyes for me were extended and the trek back to Indy was made. The furniture and other items we had transported ourselves were neatly tucked away in the moving van for this trip.

On the other end of the move, back in Indianapolis, activity was consuming our energy as well. Now it was time to locate a place to open our pending business. A great deal of thanks and numerous plaudits go to my dear dad, who always had high hopes of being an entrepreneur. (The late 1940's dad had a small business.) "Archie's Variety Store" which was in essence a radio repair store, eventually repairs included televisions, but the variety store component involved the convenience of keeping in stock items such as thread, some hardware items that were not readily available in the neighborhood and last but not least popular phonograph records. The four oldest of us children had good experience in operating a business from the clerical standpoint. With all the assistance from dad, our business was opened in the summer of 1960 and NU-LOOK TAILORS AND CLEANERS operated for the next 6 years. Circumstances beyond our control caused the demise of our business venture and some tailoring was conducted from home for another year. Necessity required my husband to seek employment elsewhere, and this led to a brief job as a health worker (a public health aide) and eventually he was recommended for the job that he retired from, which was that of being a Vocational Teacher for 25 years for the State Department of Corrections. My employment journey had continued in nursing as well as being a counter girl at the cleaners. I worked the evening shift at the hospital in order to help out at the cleaners in the morning. I really became endeared to the new concept of cooking with the electric stoves with timer ovens. My dear husband, although a very good cook, usually had only to re-heat his meals once he arrived home in the evening. This schedule continued until July 1963. At this time I made a visit to see a classmate of mine from high school and nursing at the office she now worked, and this visit turned into a job interview with a new physician who would be coming on board in this particular office. Incidentally, I would not have considered myself as being dressed for success, but the interview took place, and the doctor not being a local native, and not concerned with dressing for success, needed someone totally familiar with the lay of the land, the hospitals, and locations of other places of importance to his forth coming work. I was more or less hired on the spot. I once was introduced to a colleague of his as being his nurse, secretary, left and right hand and good friend. This working union continued for 10 ½ years. A change of lifestyle so to speak required a change of employment. However, I must mention that working for the physician (an Obstetrician) definitely had its benefits, because with his professional assistance, my husband and I became parents of our son as the result of my fourth pregnancy. Because the baby was premature, I was granted extra time off following my delivery, because he was discharged to home about the time for me to return to work following the delivery. Time marched onward rather rapidly, and soon the youngster was ready to start school, and the school of our choice did not have bus service to our neighborhood, the closest pickup area was 2 miles from home, so the decision was made for me to return to work in the hospital on the grave yard shift 11 P.M. until 7 A.M. in order to meet the bus both in the mornings and afternoons. This shift was continued for more than two years and at this time our son (the ruler of the roost) informed me that he wanted me to go to work when he and daddy went to school. Thus began the day shift of hospital nursing, which continued for the next 18 years and I retired with a total of 20 years having worked in Medical Research and Radiation-Oncology Departments.

As this journey of my memoirs draws to a close, I want it to be known that the experiences, situations, and learning opportunities were enumerable and remain close and dear to my heart. I, therefore inform the world that being "All Grown Up And Dressed In White" has been a tremendous journey not desired to be traded under any circumstances.

Carrie (Ginny Girl) Kemp

ABOUT THE AUTHOR

Ginny Girl the 'nickname' given by her daddy at an early age is better known as Carrie Genevieve Kemp. She is an African-American native of Indianapolis, IN., one of nine children born to Archie J. Smith and Bettie W. Crayton Smith (eight are still living). Her siblings consist of five girls and three boys. Her parents and one brother are deceased.

With love, sacrifice, and instillation of the value and importance of education, all of the children acquired a degree in some professional field.

She is married and the mother of one son, who is very special to his parents, especially since four other pregnancies were problem pregnancies, and subsequently he is the only living child. Her husband a native of Louisville, KY migrated to Indianapolis in 1957. They are both retired, he from being a Vocational Education Teacher (Tailoring/Sewing) at two different correctional institutions in the metropolitan area of Indianapolis, and she as a registered nurse. They have been married over 40 years, and since retiring they enjoy traveling and doing volunteer work. In addition her husband is an avid golfer.

www.ingramcontent.com/pod-product-compliance
Lightning Source LLC
Chambersburg PA
CBHW051419280526
45785CB00003B/1089